OVERHEAD TEACHING KIT

Easy Grammar Lessons For the Overhead

12 Transparencies, Reproducibles, and Fun, Interactive Lessons for Teaching Essential Grammar Skills

by Jennifer Jacobson

Illustrated by Teresa Anderko

SCHOLASTIC

PROFESSIONAL BOOKS

New York • Toronto • London • Auckland • Sydney
Mexico City • New Delhi • Hong Kong • Buenos Aires

Dedication

In memory of Lisa Blau, who created this series.

Acknowledgments

*Many thanks to Jim Becker and
Liza Charlesworth*

Teachers who wish to contact Jennifer about
her staff development programs may visit her
Web site at www.jenniferjacobson.com.

Cover art Rick Stromoski

Cover design by Norma Ortiz

Interior art by Teresa Anderko

Interior design by Sydney Wright

Easy Grammar Lessons For the Overhead text copyright © 2002
by Jennifer Jacobson.

Easy Grammar Lessons For the Overhead is produced
by becker&mayer!, Bellevue, WA for Scholastic Inc.

ISBN: 0-439-38772-8

1 2 3 4 5 6 7 8 9 10   40   09 08 06 05 04 03 02

Table of Contents

Lessons

Introduction

As young students, many of us dreaded grammar lessons in school. We might have used some sort of "primer" or boring worksheets with endless drilling exercises. These days, learning grammar is no less important, but it is a lot more fun! I've created interactive lessons that not only give your students an opportunity to construct and study the patterns, principles and rules that govern grammar in the English language, but the freedom to explore grammar usage in the context of their own lives. All you'll need to conduct these lessons in your classroom is an overhead project, a dry-erase pen, and willing students.

Each lesson includes a step-by-step plan for introducing and teaching the grammar skill, an overhead transparency, and a ready-to-reproduce blackline master. We have also provided a list of literature links, and ideas for extending the skills beyond the scope of the lesson.

All best wishes to you and your students as you explore the wonders and fun of grammar!

—*Jennifer Jacobson*

Helpful Hints

- Incorporate grammar instruction into your reading and writing routine. These lessons work well as reading or writing mini-lessons.

- Select a word from a book that you are currently reading as a class when asked to choose a word or a sentence. You might invite students to search for examples from their own writing.

- Examine student writing to determine which rules of grammar you wish to focus on next. Divide students into small groups to focus on individual needs.

- Remember to focus on student thinking while doing these activities. Grammar usage is a conceptual process.

- Bring joy to your study of parts of speech. Think of it as word play! If you take on the attitude that words are delightful to work with, so will your students.

Lessons

Capitalizing Proper Nouns

Directions

1. Introduce the lesson by writing your name on the board with all lower-case letters. Then ask students what's wrong with what you wrote. Begin a discussion about how most proper nouns, such as first names, always begin with capital letters.

2. Place the transparency on the overhead projector. Write a sentence in the box that uses the same word twice: once as a common noun and once as a proper noun. Underline the word you chose. For example: My favorite <u>park</u> is Central <u>Park</u>.

3. Point to the underlined words and ask, "Why is the word *park* capitalized in one place and not in the other?"

4. Guide students to understand that a word can be either a common noun or a proper noun, depending on how it is used.

5. Write a few common nouns in the left column that represent places or people, such as *teacher* and *school*. Ask students to give you proper nouns that identify each of the common nouns, such as *Ms. Simmons* and *Lincoln School*. Write their responses in the right-hand column. Then reverse the procedure by first filling in proper nouns.

6. Remind students that asking themselves, "Does this word name a *particular* person, place, or thing?" will help them to remember whether or not the word needs to be capitalized.

To Extend the Lesson

❋ Provide different themes for each student, such as the zoo, neighborhoods, and favorite books or movies, or let students choose their own theme. Copy and distribute the blackline master, and have each student fill in common and proper nouns that go with their theme. Then have each student write a story on their theme, using the common and proper nouns they have listed. Afterwards, students can share their stories with the whole class.

Capitalizing Proper Nouns

common nouns	proper nouns

Plural Nouns

☼ Skills ☼ Addressed

- Mastering the spelling of singular and plural nouns: *–s, –es, –ies, –ves*
- Identifying collective nouns

☼ Purpose ☼

In this lesson, students learn to recognize singular and plural nouns and to review spelling changes.

☼ Literature ☼ Links

Merry Go Round: A Book About Nouns and A Cache of Jewels and Other Collective Nouns, by Ruth Heller

A Pinky is a Baby Mouse, by Pamela Munoz Ryan

Directions

1. In preparation for your lesson on plural nouns, remind students that a noun is a name for a person, place, or thing. Have students provide a list of nouns from around the classroom. Write them on the board.

2. Place the transparency on the overhead projector. Cover the scoreboard with a sheet of paper. Ask a volunteer to choose one word from the list of nouns you compiled. Write the noun, one letter in each box, along the top of the grid.

3. Tell students that nouns can be written as singular nouns, which represent one thing, or plural nouns, which represent more than one thing. Identify the noun you wrote as plural or singular.

4. Invite students to provide singular nouns that begin with each letter written across the top of your grid. For example, if the noun written across is *book*, students will have to think of a singular noun that begins with the letter *b*, such as *bear*. Write these singular nouns in the correct column.

5. Now ask students to give you the plural form of each of the nouns you just wrote. For example, the plural form of bear is *bears*. Review the rules for adding *-s* and *-es*, changing *-y* to *-i* and adding *-es*, creating collective nouns, and changing *-f* to *-ves*.

6. Uncover the scorecard. Help students determine their score based on the rules they needed to follow when listing the plural nouns.

To Extend the Lesson

❈ Copy and distribute the blackline master. Divide the class into pairs, and give each pair a copy of a book you are reading in class. Have one member of the pair pick a word from the book to write across the top of the grid. The other member of the pair will then have to fill in the columns with singular and plural nouns. After the first member is finished, the pairs switch roles. The one with the highest score at the end is the team winner!

Plural Nouns

singular nouns											
plural nouns											
points											

score board	
add *s*	1 point
add *es*	2 points
change *y* to *i* add *es*	5 points
collective noun	5 points
change *f* to *ves*	10 points

Class Total:

Past Tense Verbs

◎ Skills ◎
Addressed

- Distinguishing between present and past tense
- Spelling the past tense of regular verbs; using –d and –ed
- Choosing vivid, precise verbs when writing

◎ Purpose ◎

In this lesson, students learn that verbs can be written in present or past tense, and that writers use precise verbs to make their writing strong and vivid.

◎ Literature ◎
Links

Bear Snores On, by Karma Wilson

Faraway Home, by Jane Kurtz

Directions

1. Tell students that good writers pay close attention to verbs. They know that choosing the most clear or precise verb can turn so-so writing into exceptional writing. Write the sentence "I ate popcorn" on the board. Explain that this sentence would be very different if we replaced the verb *ate* with verbs like *chewed, gobbled,* and *munched*. Have students think of other verbs that would make this sentence more appealing.

2. Place the transparency on the overhead projector. Write a sentence in the present tense on the bottom line, such as, *I walk to the store*.

3. Remind students that a verb is a word that tells an action. Ask, "What is the verb in this sentence?" Circle the verb.

4. Continue by saying that a verb can be written to tell about an action that is happening right now, in the present, or an action that has already happened, in the past. Help students determine whether the verb in your sentence was written in the past or the present tense.

5. Write the verb *walk* in the center circle of the diagram. Ask students to suggest synonyms for the word walk. Ask, "How might I have walked? Show me." Invite students to demonstrate different ways of walking and have others choose words that describe the actions.

6. Write these present-tense verbs in the next circle. Then ask students to give you these verbs in past tense. Write these verbs in the outer circle. Discuss the rules for adding -*ed* and -*d*, doubling consonants and adding -*ed*, and changing -*y* to -*i* and adding -*ed*.

7. Point out and circle irregular verbs such as *run* and *ran*. Have students finish by picking out one of the new verbs to put in your sentence.

To Extend the Lesson

❂ Copy and distribute the blackline master. Have each student think of an activity they enjoy, such as softball, reading, or playing a musical instrument. Let them come up with a sentence that shows their action during this activity (encourage them to pick a dull, typical verb, such as "I play the trumpet"). They write the verb from their sentence in the middle circle, and pass their paper to the front of the room. Then distribute the papers randomly, making sure that the owner does not get his or her paper. Have students fill in the diagram, using what they now know about past tense and precise verbs.

Past Tense Verbs

Helping Verbs

Directions

1. Begin by engaging students in a discussion about helping verbs. On the board, you might write the sentence "I am speaking to you." Then ask students which word in the sentence is the helping verb. Review with them that helping verbs show whether something is happening in the present tense or the past tense. In this case, the word *am* helps the reader know that the action is in the present tense.

2. Place the transparency on the overhead projector. Write a sentence that includes the helping verb *am* and a main verb with *-ing* on the line at the top. For example, *I am hiking*. Point out that this sentence has a verb, "hike" and a helping verb, "am."

3. Ask students to think of other verbs that could describe a hike up a mountain such as *climbing, leaping, stumbling, scrambling, groping, slipping,* and *reaching*. Write the words that students suggest in the word box at the bottom.

4. Encourage students to work in pairs or small groups to arrange the verbs in a story-telling poem. Explain that each line should begin: *I am,* and end with one of the verbs written in the box. Then come back together to record the poetry on the transparency.

5. Read one of the poems again, but substitute the word *was* for *am*. Guide students to see that *was* is a helping verb that indicates past tense.

To Extend the Lesson

✿ Copy and distribute the blackline master. Encourage students to write their own poems, choosing different main and helping verbs. Challenge them to begin with quieter verbs such as *reading, writing, sleeping* or *smiling,* and end with noisy verbs, such as *pounding, stomping, singing,* or *laughing*.

✿ Play a game of charades! In this game, the students trying to guess the action must call out using helping verbs, such as "You are driving a car," or "You are cooking dinner."

❂ Skills ❂ Addressed

- Helping verbs
- Adding *-ing* to verbs

❂ Purpose ❂

In this lesson, students discover helping verbs, and review spelling rules for adding *-ing* to regular verbs.

❂ Literature ❂ Links

Kites Sail High: A Book About Verbs, by Ruth Heller

Weslandia (to explore present tense), by Paul Fleishman

Helping Verbs

_____

Word Box

Comparative Adjective Chart

Directions

1. In advance, gather three different-sized balls, such as a tennis ball, a kick ball, and a volleyball. Begin by displaying the balls at the front of the room. Hold up the tennis ball first and say, "This is a big ball." Then hold up the kick ball and say, "This is a bigger ball." When you hold up the volleyball say, "This is the biggest ball." As you say *big, bigger,* and *biggest,* write the words on the board, underlining the different endings. Explain that you will be practicing how to add different endings to adjectives, to show comparison.

2. Remind students that an adjective describes a noun. Ask students to give you examples of different adjectives. Write these on the board. Then place the transparency on the overhead projector.

3. Tell students that there are three kinds of adjectives: *positive, comparative,* and *superlative.* Choose one of the adjectives students called out and use the word in a sentence, for example: *This dog is smart.* Write this sentence on the top line of the transparency. Tell students that *smart* is a *positive* adjective, and write it in the first column of the chart.

4. Write sentences using the other two adjective forms, *smarter* (comparative) and *smartest* (superlative), and place the adjectives in the correct columns on the chart.

5. Ask students to name other adjectives and add them to the chart. As you record the words, ask students to tell you the rules that govern how to write the word endings. Record the rules, such as changing a -y ending to -i before adding -er or -est, in the box at the bottom of the transparency.

6. Guide students to understand that some adjectives do not follow the pattern. Adjectives such as *beautiful, famous,* and *charming* require the words *more* and *most* or *less* and *least* for making comparisons. Brainstorm other adjectives that don't follow the pattern. Write them in the ribbon. Other words, such as *good,* follow a whole other pattern. Challenge students to give you the comparative (*better*) and superlative (*best*) of this word.

To Extend the Lesson

❂ Make a class superlatives book. Similar to a yearbook that includes a section with the "smartest, tallest, and most athletic," create labels for each student in your class. So there are no hurt feelings, keep the labels objective, such as tallest, shortest, longest hair, lives closest to school, and so on. Students can illustrate their page in the book. Keep the finished product in your book area.

Comparative Adjective Chart

_____

_____

_____

positive	comparative	superlative

Words that need <u>least</u> or <u>more</u>

Spelling Rule Box

Adverbs

☼ Skills ☼ Addressed

• Definition of adverb

☼ Purpose ☼

In this lesson, students begin to understand the definition and use of adverbs.

☼ Literature ☼ Links

Yard Sale!, by Mitra Modarressi

Up, Up and Away: A Book About Adverbs, by Ruth Heller

Directions

1   Explain to students that you will be discussing adverbs. Tell them that adverbs tell how, when, or where an action takes place.

2   Place the transparency on the overhead projector. Write the following three sentences at the top of the overlay:

> I painted carefully.
> Yesterday I painted.
> I painted upstairs.

3   Circle the adverbs in each sentence. Point out that one sentence describes *how* I painted, one describes *when* I painted, and the third describes *where* I painted.

4   Write a verb (past tense) in the center circle of the transparency. Ask a volunteer to give you an adverb that modifies (or tells more about) that verb. Have him or her tell you in which circle the adverb should be placed. Then ask the volunteer to use the verb and the adverb in a sentence.

5   Continue with this verb until all three circles are filled. Then erase the transparency and repeat the activity using different verbs. Ask students to complete the circles without repeating adverbs.

6   Students may quickly realize that words with the ending *-ly* are adverbs. Challenge them to come up with "how" adverbs that do not have an -ly, such as *fast* or *well*.

7   You may find that students confuse "where" adverbs with prepositional phrases. For example, a student might offer, "I painted <u>in the garage</u>," as opposed to "I painted <u>nearby</u>." Tell students to pick a *single* word as their adverb.

To Extend the Lesson

✪   Copy and distribute the blackline master. Invite students to fill in the spaces using verbs from their favorite books or movies. For example, if the book is *Charlotte's Web*, they might write the following sentences: *Templeton ran through the fairground <u>greedily</u>, Templeton raced <u>out</u>,* and *Templeton searched for food <u>later</u>.* Add the adverbs they create to your class word board.

Adverbs

_____

_____

_____

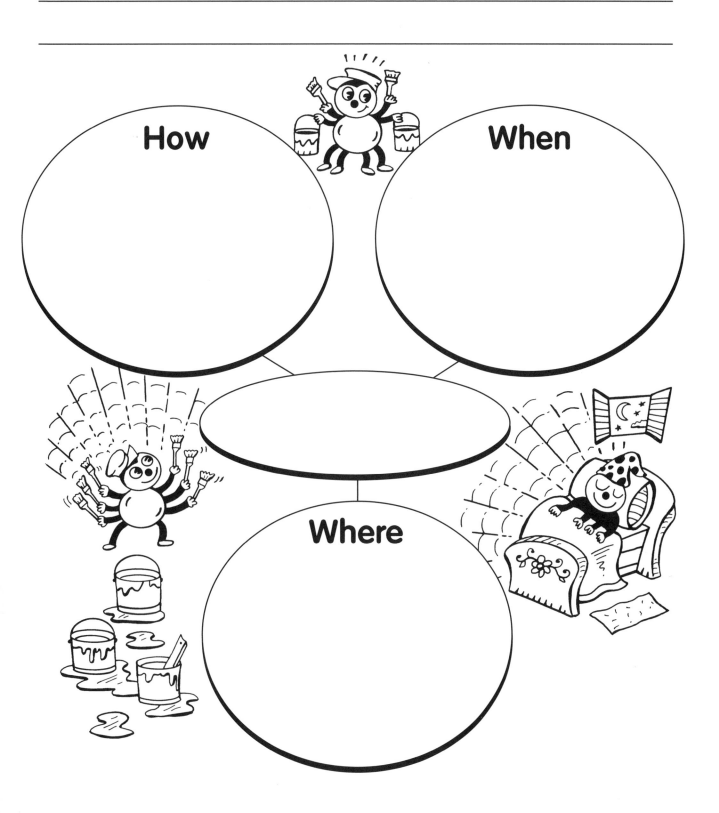

How

When

Where

Sorting Parts of Speech

Directions

1. Now that you have reviewed nouns, verbs, adjectives, and adverbs, it's time to pull all of them together. Write the following sentence on the board: *The crowd was noisy.* Ask, "What type of word, or part of speech, is the word *crowd*?" (noun)

2. Now write this sentence: *"Don't crowd me," I said.* Ask, "What type of word, or part of speech, is the word *crowd*?" (verb) When students answer you correctly, say, "But I thought you told me it was a noun."

3. Guide students to tell you that a word can have different jobs in different sentences. Validate their thinking by writing this sentence on the board: *The crowded room was filled.* Ask, "What part of speech is the word *crowded*, which comes from the base word *crowd*, in this sentence?" (adjective)

4. Place the transparency on the overhead projector. Ask students to take turns giving you sentences. Write one sentence at a time at the top of the page.

5. Ask students, "Do you see a noun in this sentence? A verb?" Have students tell you in which can to sort the words. Continue until you have sorted as many nouns, verbs, adjectives, and adverbs as possible.

6. As you repeat the exercise, students will try to come up with sentences that include both adjectives and adverbs, such as *The plaid kite flew briskly*, giving them many opportunities to recall the definition and uses of parts of speech.

7. Some students may come up with sentences that include more than one of each of the parts of speech. Challenge them with sentences like these: *My frustrated dog dug the earth wildly, quickly found the brittle bone, and devoured it momentarily.*

To Extend the Lesson

✪ Copy and distribute the blackline master. Encourage students to write their own "Mad Libs." Have them write brief stories, leaving one word (noun, verb, adjective, or adverb) missing from each sentence, and replace it with a blank line. Below the line, have students write the part of speech necessary to complete the sentence, and have students pass their stories to their classmates to fill in. Students then read their stories to the class.

❂ Skills ❂ Addressed

- Using context to determine parts of speech
- Identifying nouns, verbs, adjectives and adverbs

❂ Purpose ❂

In this lesson, students learn that words can be different parts of speech depending on their location and job in a sentence.

❂ Literature ❂ Links

Wow! It's Great Being A Duck, by Joan Rankin

Bootsie Barker Bites, by Barbara Bottner

Sorting Parts of Speech

Nouns

Verbs

Adjectives

Adverbs

Mixed-Up Sentences

Skills Addressed

- Recognizing subject and predicate
- Identifying a complete sentence

Purpose

In this lesson, students learn that a complete sentence must have a subject and a predicate.

Literature Links

The Dinosaurs of Waterhouse Hawkins, by Barbara Kerley

Nature Wild and Wonderful, by Laurence Pringle

Directions

1. Begin the lesson by asking volunteers to help you write a sentence on the board. Tell students that a sentence is a group of words that tell a complete thought. Sentences have a subject, such as "the girl," that tells *who* or *what* the sentence is about. If the sentence you write on the board is *The girl played the piano*, ask, "Who is this sentence about?" Circle the word "girl." Then tell students that sentences also have a predicate. The predicate tells about the subject. Ask, "What word or words tells about the subject?" Circle the words "played the piano."

2. Place the transparency on the overhead projector. Ask students to help you write a short sentence in the box at the bottom, such as, *The rabbit hopped across the grass*. Review how to pick out the subjects and predicates in a sentence. Have students identify them, and then write them in the appropriate boxes on the transparency.

3. Erase the first sentence (leaving the subject and predicate in the boxes) and encourage students to give you additional sentences. Remind them that sentences can begin in a variety of interesting ways. If students seem stuck in their beginnings, have them search for interesting sentences in the books they're reading.

4. Determine the subject and predicate for each new sentence and write them in the appropriate boxes.

5. Write your own incomplete sentence such as: *Went to town*. After students have attempted to dissect the sentence, point out that this phrase is not a sentence. Remind them that a sentence must have a subject and a predicate to be complete.

6. Challenge students to give you the shortest complete sentence possible. Show them that a sentence can be just two words: *She smiled*.

To Extend the Lesson

- Copy and distribute the blackline master. Divide the class into two groups. Have one group write only subjects, and one group write only predicates. Then, have the groups come together and make up unusual sentences, joining subjects with unmatching predicates, such as *Spotted lizards played the piano*.

Mixed-Up Sentences

Subjects

Predicates

Complete Sentences

Contractions!

Directions

1 Explain that today, you are going to practice making and writing contractions, which consist of two words that combine to become one, with the help of an apostrophe.

2 Place the transparency on the overhead projector. Write a few root words in the left-hand beaker (such as *did, do, would, she,* and *let*), and a few typical contraction words in the right-hand beaker (such as *us, not, will, have,* and *are*). Make sure that each word on the left has a match on the right!

3 Point out that by combining words in the left-hand beaker with words in the right-hand beaker, students can create contractions. Model how to make a contraction by combining *did* and *not* to create *didn't*.

4 As you combine the words, discuss how to use the apostrophe. Say, "Use an apostrophe in place of the letters that are left out."

5 Ask students to tell you two words that combine to make a contraction and to spell the word for you. Write the word in the glass jar. As you continue, occasionally ask, "How did you know where to put the apostrophe?"

6 Take time to discuss difficult contractions such as *won't* and *I'd.* You might also mention that students often write "should of" when they mean to write *should've.*

7 Point out that writers use contractions when their writing is relaxed and friendly. In more formal types of writing, writers usually use the two words instead of contractions.

To Extend the Lesson

✹ Copy and distribute the blackline master, and encourage students to fill it in with other contractions they read or hear in conversation. They should pull it apart before writing the whole word in the jar.

✹ Let students invent and decorate bumper stickers with contractions, such as *"I'd rather be reading,"* or *"Honk if you're happy!"*

Contractions!

Signs, Signs, Everywhere are Signs! (with apostrophes)

◎ Skills ◎ Addressed

- Using apostrophes with possessive nouns
- Differentiating between contractions and possessives

◎ Purpose ◎

In this lesson students learn to recognize possessive nouns and to use an apostrophe correctly.

◎ Literature ◎ Links

Ginger's House, by Catherine Stock

Painting the Wind: A Story of Vincent van Gogh, by Michelle Dionetti

Directions

1. In advance, make a simple sign that shows possession, such as "[your name]'s House" or "Rover's Dog House." Start a discussion about what these signs have in common. Ask, "Why is there an apostrophe before the *s*?" Tell students that a noun showing ownership is a possessive noun.

2. Place the transparency on the overhead. Make a sign in one of the sign shapes, such as *Joe's Hat Shop*.

3. Guide students to understand that apostrophes show that something belongs to someone. In this case, the hat shop belongs to Joe.

4. Encourage students to provide other messages that might appear on signs showing possession. You might suggest that they use their own name, but not the names of classmates. Encourage them to create a variety of texts such as *Order Bessie's Pie!*, *Your Pet's Favorite Store*, and *A Kid's Place*.

5. Explain that there are some instances when possessives can be confused with contractions. Erase what you've written on the transparency so far and make the following sign: *Tomorrow's the Last Day of This Sale!*

6. Ask students to tell you if the message shows possession or whether it contains a contraction. Suggest that students try to read the word as two words to see if it is a contraction.

7. For extra challenge, create a sign on the transparency, leaving out the apostrophe. Let students tell you where the apostrophe goes, if it's needed.

To Extend the Lesson

❂ If your class is ready, repeat this activity at another time, creating signs that use plural possessives, such as *Read the Three Students' Essays Inside*, and *Many Players' Hats Are on Display*.

❂ Copy and distribute the blackline master. Divide the class into pairs. Have each student in a group create signs on their paper, leaving off the apostrophes. They then switch papers with their partner and must add the apostrophes where needed. Afterwards, bring the class together again to review the rules and correct any mistakes.

Signs, Signs, Everywhere are Signs!

(with apostrophes)

Commas on the Menu

Directions

1. Place the transparency on the overhead projector.

2. Ask students to imagine that they've just come to the most wonderful restaurant. Invite them to name some of their favorite foods that would be found on the menu. Write all responses on the transparency, under the appropriate headings.

3. Next, write a sentence on the board that tells what items you would order from this restaurant, but leave out the commas. For example,

   I will have lobster salad rolls and lemonade.

4. Ask, "What is it that I will be having?" Guide students to debate whether you will be having lobster with a side salad or a lobster salad. Tell students that commas are needed to make sense of this sentence.

5. Point out that commas are used to separate items in a list or series. Demonstrate how to punctuate your sentence:

   I will have lobster, salad, rolls, and lemonade.

6. Ask student to dictate sentences that tell what they would order from the menu. Have them tell you where to place the commas; for example, saying "I will have a hot dog *comma* potato chips *comma* a cookie *comma* and milk" will help them remember to use commas when writing lists. Write their sentences on the board.

7. Choose a point to stop asking verbally what a student wishes to order. Instead, write on the board, "Susan, what would you like to order?"

8. Repeat this exercise for the next few students and then ask, "Do any of you see a new use for the comma?" Help students recognize that we use a comma to set off the names of people who are spoken to directly.

To Extend the Lesson

- Copy and distribute the blackline master. Have students fill in each menu section with silly foods, such as gizzard goop, bird beans, and bear bananas. Then have them create stories about people ordering these different foods in a restaurant. They can illustrate the stories and read them aloud to the whole class.

Commas on the Menu

Menu

Appetizers

Main Dishes

Menu

Side Orders

Desserts

Beverages

Conversational Quotation Marks

Skills Addressed

- Quotation marks
- Conventions of written dialogue

Purpose

In this lesson, students learn the rules that govern the use of quotation marks in written conversations.

Literature Links

Lilly's Purple Plastic Purse, by Kevin Henkes

Guess How Much I Love You, by Sam McBratney

Directions

1. Tell students that dialogue is what happens when two or more people talk within a story. Read them an example of dialogue from a favorite book. Then have groups of students select two or three interesting lines of dialogue from the book they are currently reading.

2. Place the transparency on the overhead projector. Have groups dictate snippets of dialogue to you. Write each exchange, with commas and proper capitalization—but without quotation marks—on the transparency. For example:

   > Tonya asked, Have your read about Big Foot?
   > I've never heard of Big Foot, said David.

3. Point out to students that when writers create dialogue, they begin a new paragraph each time a new person speaks.

4. Tell students that when people talk in stories, quotation marks show the exact words a person says. Demonstrate how to form quotation marks. Then, ask volunteers to come up to the overhead and put quotation marks in the correct places in each sentence.

5. Erase the dialogue you have written so far. Write patterns of dialogue using lines and punctuation as follows:

   _____, "_____."
   "_____?" _____.
   "_____!"

6. Invite students to make up dialogue that would fit the templates you created.

To Extend the Lesson

- Copy and distribute the blackline master. Tell students that writers learn a lot about people by listening to and recording conversations. Have students make up a conversation on their copy of the blackline master, perhaps between themselves and their friends, families, or even you! Encourage them to get the words down first. Then they can return to what they wrote to add the proper punctuation.

Conversational Quotation Marks

Notes

Notes

Notes